IF

MW01136289

Greater Than a Tourist Book Series
Reviews from Readers

I think the series is wonderful and beneficial for tourists to get information before visiting the city.

-Seckin Zumbul, Izmir Turkey

I am a world traveler who has read many trip guides but this one really made a difference for me. I would call it a heartfelt creation of a local guide expert instead of just a guide.

-Susy, Isla Holbox, Mexico

New to the area like me, this is a must have!

-Joe, Bloomington, USA

This is a good series that gets down to it when looking for things to do at your destination without having to read a novel for just a few ideas.

-Rachel, Monterey, USA

i

Good information to have to plan my trip to this destination.

-Pennie Farrell, Mexico

Great ideas for a port day.

-Mary Martin USA

Aptly titled, you won't just be a tourist after reading this book. You'll be greater than a tourist!

-Alan Warner, Grand Rapids, USA

Even though I only have three days to spend in San Miguel in an upcoming visit, I will use the author's suggestions to guide some of my time there. An easy read - with chapters named to guide me in directions I want to go.

 -Robert Catapano, USA

Great insights from a local perspective! Useful information and a very good value!

 -Sarah, USA

This series provides an in-depth experience through the eyes of a local. Reading these series will help you to travel the city in with confidence and it'll make your journey a unique one.

-Andrew Teoh, Ipoh, Malaysia

GREATER THAN A TOURIST- BOISE IDAHO USA

50 Travel Tips from a Local

Dylan Cade

The statements in this book are of the authors and may not be the views of
CZYK Publishing or Greater Than a Tourist.

Cover designed by: Ivana Stamenkovic
Cover Image: https://pixabay.com/en/boise-idaho-panorama-city-winter-
3593888/

CZYK Publishing Since 2011.

Greater Than a Tourist
Visit our website at www.GreaterThanaTourist.com

Lock Haven, PA
All rights reserved.
ISBN: 9781791610791

>TOURIST

50 TRAVEL TIPS FROM A LOCAL

BOOK DESCRIPTION

Are you excited about planning your next trip?

Do you want to try something new?

Would you like some guidance from a local?

If you answered yes to any of these questions, then this Greater Than a Tourist book is for you.

Greater Than a Tourist - Boise, Idaho, U.S.A by Dylan Cade offers the inside scoop on Boise. Most travel books tell you how to travel like a tourist. Although there is nothing wrong with that, as part of the Greater Than a Tourist series, this book will give you travel tips from someone who has lived at your next travel destination.

In these pages, you will discover advice that will help you throughout your stay. This book will not tell you exact addresses or store hours but instead will give you excitement and knowledge from a local that you may not find in other smaller print travel books.

Travel like a local. Slow down, stay in one place, and get to know the people and the culture. By the time you finish this book, you will be eager and prepared to travel to your next destination.

TABLE OF CONTENTS

DEDICATION

This book is dedicated to GBC, who showed me the joy of discovery.

ABOUT THE AUTHOR

I moved to Boise with my parents in 1997 when I was just two years old. Growing up there, I spent most of my time in Southeast Boise but have lived or played in just about every part of town, exploring the wilderness nearby with my friends. Through college I spent time rock climbing on the cliffs nearby, checking out bars and restaurants, and driving off the beaten track to some of the out-of-the-way highlights of Idaho.

As a teenager I thought that Boise was just about the most boring place in the world. It wasn't until I traveled the world during and after college that I saw just how unique and rare of a place it is. I came to miss the time I could spend outdoors and the personality of my favorite places. The way people treat each other, the natural sights, the positive energy and the dynamic outdoor scene all come together to make Boise special.

HOW TO USE THIS BOOK

The Greater Than a Tourist book series was written by someone who has lived in an area for over three months. The goal of this book is to help travelers either dream or experience different locations by providing opinions from a local. The author has made suggestions based on their own experiences. Please do your own research before traveling to the area in case the suggested places are unavailable.

Travel Advisories: As a first step in planning any trip abroad, check the Travel Advisories for your intended destination.
https://travel.state.gov/content/travel/en/traveladvisories/traveladvisories.html

FROM THE PUBLISHER

Traveling can be one of the most important parts of a person's life. The anticipation and memories that you have are some of the best. As a publisher of the Greater Than a Tourist book series, as well as the popular 50 Things to Know book series, we strive to help you learn about new places, spark your imagination, and inspire you. Wherever you are and whatever you do I wish you safe, fun, and inspiring travel.

Lisa Rusczyk Ed. D.
CZYK Publishing

OUR STORY

Traveling is a passion of the "Greater than a Tourist" series creator. Lisa studied abroad in college, and for their honeymoon Lisa and her husband toured Europe. During her travels to Malta, an older man tried to give her some advice based on his own experience living on the island since he was a young boy. She was not sure if she should talk to the stranger but was interested in his advice. When traveling to some places she was wary to talk to locals because she was afraid that they weren't being genuine. Through her travels, Lisa learned how much locals had to share with tourists. Lisa created the "Greater Than a Tourist" book series to help connect people with locals. A topic that locals are very passionate about sharing.

WELCOME TO
> TOURIST

INTRODUCTION

"Not only until we are lost do we begin to understand ourselves" - Henry David Thoreau

Idaho is wild country. Even more than 150 years after the settlers from the East made their way, much of the countryside is untouched and scarcely traveled. It's a place for those looking to see the fabled natural beauty of America and the untamed wilderness. It's the home of geological anomalies: hot springs, fault lines, canyons, and cliffs criss-cross a state where practically every biome but the tropical is represented.

Boise is like the rest of Idaho but slower. The city earned its name from French fur trappers in the 1800's, who could not help but exclaim "les bois, regarde les bois!" ("the woods, look at the woods!") over the first real forest for miles around. Boise sits on a leafy river over a deep watershed, with mesas to either side and mountains beyond that. Animals still live amongst the parks and suburbs. It's a soft place where people lead quiet lives, but it's beginning to put itself on the map with new festivals, restaurants, and artists, attracting more and more people to come to Boise and start families and careers. The city has grown rapidly. The population has increased by 100,000 people since 1990 and shows signs of accelerating. To me, it still feels like the city sits outside of time and only changes half as much as the rest of the world, and that's what I like about it. When you go, give yourself lots of free time to spend getting lost in the corners and the alleyways.

1. WHY AM I HERE?

Boise is out of the way. There's no denying it. Many people fly right over Idaho to the more glamorous and populous cities of the West Coast, but there is a timeless charm to Idaho that is worth exploring. If you're interested in seeing the best of the outdoors that the United States has to offer, then that's why you're in Idaho. Known for some of the best mountain biking, river kayaking, skiing, and rock climbing in the world, Idaho is a diamond in the rough. Boise represents the civic heart of wild Idaho; friendly but a bit rambunctious at times with that characteristic country friendliness. Nestled between two mountain ranges in the Treasure Valley and split by the Boise River, Boise is a warm and well-developed town with easy access to the surrounding wilderness.

These days, Boise has a lot to offer—more than it did 20 years ago. The town has been growing rapidly as folks disillusioned with life in the bigger cities nearby seek a quieter life. Civic engagement from newcomers has been mixing with the style and character of the locals, sparking new projects and events while expanding on existing ones. I don't know how long Boise is going to keep its rural charm, so go and see it now while it's at its best.

2. WHAT'S THAT BIG CROSS UP THERE?

Well assuming you know what it's referencing, you're probably asking why its on this particular hill. In 1956, a Christian missionary group called the Jaycee Club paid $880 to erect the cross at Tablerock as a testament to what they believed was a central characteristic of the Idahoan identity at the time: they thought that the cross was a symbol of American character in contrast to atheist communism. In a way, it's a Cold War Monument that portrays the patriotic sentiments of Idahoans at the time, but many attempts to remove the cross since have been foiled, indicating that it retains some importance in the minds of many Idaho citizens. Idaho is a traditional and politically conservative state, with several different religious affiliation, most of which are derived from Christianity, and the cross tends to overemphasize these features to visitors. The cross is a privately owned piece of property that will probably remain for years to come, but the City of Boise is accepting, laid-back, and casually friendly to all kinds of people. If you want a closer look, the trailhead to Tablerock is behind the Old Idaho Penitentiary.

3. GETTING AROUND

Boise has a fairly developed public transportation system. Mostly for commuters, it services downtown and out into the surrounding towns up to Caldwell, which is 45 minutes west of downtown, but has useful services down Parkcenter Boulevard (along the Boise River), and up into the Hill Road Mesas in the North End. You will also find a bus moving up State Street into Garden City and the older parts of town. State Street is mostly home to old housing and frankly dilapidated businesses, relics of the 60's and 70's, but also a few of the undiscovered gems of the city.

If you're determined to explore outside of the city (which you really should do), a car is the best option for transportation. Access to a number of trailheads, out-of-the-way businesses, and day trips is dependent on having a car. The city is easy to navigate, but drivers should be aware of the network of one-way streets criss-crossing downtown, as these can sometimes be confusing. The Boise Airport hosts several different rental car agencies, with several agencies on-site and frequent shuttles to off-site locations. Having used the on-site rental car service before, I can attest to its convenience.

4.PARKING

Parking in the city is a breeze. There is hardly ever a lack of spaces, especially during the day, and if you are willing to park a few blocks from your destination you might find free two-hour or four-hour parking. Between 6th and 2nd avenues, east of downtown, there are whole streets of free parking. The garages downtown also collectively allow free parking for one hour except during special events, and many restaurants and businesses like the Edwards 9 movie theater provide parking validation. Metered parking in the city is generally inexpensive and is free on Sundays and holidays.

If you're heading to a popular hiking or outdoors spot on a spring or summer weekend, you might encounter trouble finding convenient parking, but if you're willing to walk a little farther there's usually a line of cars along the road. Feel free to join them and you won't be ticketed.

5. WHERE TO STAY

A person traveling in Idaho has a number of choices when picking their home base. Whether staying in the city or in the country, there are lodges, hotels, and Airbnb's.

If you're looking to stay in Boise, the most upscale places to stay are the Grove Hotel, the Modern Hotel and Bar, and the Inn at 500 Capitol. These hotels emphasize quality and class for a higher price tag, as well as great locations downtown.

For the whimsically-minded, the Anniversary Inn near the Train Depot showcases unique rooms of various themes from Roman palace to safari to pirate ship. Its suites are full of personality and are suitable for couples and families looking for a Disney-style room.

For middle-priced options there's the Safari Inn, a staple in a convenient location downtown, and the Stay Alfred at The Fowler, a new hotel near the Boise Zoo garnering a good reputation.

In previous decades a cheaper option would have meant choosing a motel, but nowadays you can find a number of Airbnb's. The better choices are around $40-60 and nestled near downtown and are available as apartments or as single rooms for the solo traveler.

Although you will have to clean up after yourself, Airbnb's are a great way to experience convenience and freedom.

6. REMEMBER TO BRING

In the summer, remember to bring some good walking shoes or boots, your favorite hat, a pair of sunglasses, a beach towel (no, really), swimwear, and some ziploc bags. It might also be wise to buy or bring sunscreen, as the summer sun can be intense. If you're heading there in the winter, still bring the sunglasses, some long underwear for layers and your own goggles if you're going to be skiing or sledding. It's just more comfortable that way.

7. SOCIAL MEDIA GROUPS

Check out Facebook to connect with the Visit Idaho and Visit Boise pages, both of which are updated daily with articles, photos, and tips for people planning a trip or already there. If looking to field a general request or question about visiting, these groups are where to ask.

8. BLEND WITH THE LOCALS

Everyone in Boise knows how to spot a tourist by the way they say Boise. If you've grown up there, you probably say "Boy-see," and if you're from out-of-town, you most likely have heard it pronounced Boy-zee. Nobody is going to correct you and it doesn't matter at all but we love talking about it.

It may not be noticeable because the people of Boise are a cheerful sort, but the city people are a quiet sort. Obviously bars and clubs are an exception, but people generally keep it pretty reserved around the city and making too much noise is considered rude, especially if you're swearing and cursing and hollering. If you're on 8th street at night you can practically ignore this rule, but during the day people like to cultivate peace and calm. Notable exceptions are when rafting the river, because people generally expect rafters to go crazy, and BSU game days.

9. WHERE TO BUY GROCERIES

If you're staying in an Airbnb or a suite with a kitchen, you have more freedom to cook for yourself. Downtown has a few different kinds of grocery

21

stores. For all the regular stuff, the easiest spots are Winco and Whole Foods, which represent the two ends of the price spectrum. Aside from that, there is a Fred Meyer's on Federal Way that has everything under the sun, several Albertsons (a middle-priced Northwest chain), and an asian grocery on Overland Road called TradeViet that has ingredients that other stores don't carry. It's worth mentioning that the Boise Farmers' Market, open on Saturday mornings from April to October, has the freshest and most delicious produce, meats, and breads, and I stress that a visit there would be worthwhile to someone looking to make an artisan meal.

10. THE FARMERS' MARKET

Boise's farmers' market is only open on Saturday mornings from 8 a.m. to noon from May to October. It's unique in that there is only one in the city, and everyone goes to that one. It used to be only the same two dozens vendors along 8th street, but now it's expanded to take up more than two city blocks and four streets! It's really the perfect place to buy souvenirs or sample some local Idaho delicacies like huckleberry jam, elderberry wine, or some scrumptious local cheeses. My favorite morning activity is getting in line at the cartoonish donut-flipping-machine and keeping my hands warm with fresh-fried mini donuts.

11. IDAHO POTATOES AREN'T IN IDAHO

Now before you get all excited about it, you really ought to know that if you've come all this way to Idaho for an Idaho potato then you should just turn around and go to France. All of our famous Idaho potatoes are shipped out to other places to enjoy; as Idaho's main export (other than beef and corn), the potatoes are sought after worldwide and can be extremely difficult to find in-state. However, I know a place in Boise that sells Idaho souvenirs, and if you ask nicely, they might just sell you a single potato instead of their usual half dozen (wrapped in gold foil). The store is called Spuds, near the Grove on 8th street, and they have quite a few knicks and knacks besides.

12. BREAKFAST SPOTS

Boise has a love affair with breakfast that is rivaled by no one. Idaho is the diner breakfast personified: when you imagine wandering into town from the dusty road, looking for a pot of coffee and a stupefyingly delicious pie, that's Idaho. My favorite places are, in no particular order:

The Chef's Hut. A classic, run-of-the-mill diner, the kind that will absolutely knock your socks off. Their hash browns are sublime, their coffee to die for, the pancakes light and fluffy. It's one of my favorite spots in town, notable for its proximity to ABU Games and the Edwards 21 movie theater. The place closes at 2 p.m., so don't dawdle.

Moon's Kitchen Cafe has traded ownership about 3 times in the last twenty years, but their food has stayed solid. Moon's has a laid-back country atmosphere, a friendly staff, and is a great place to catch an omelette or just burgers and fries.

Despite its location among the other boutiques of Bowne Crossing, Locavore is affordable. Sporting high quality local ingredients and a lovely selection of wines, Locavore represents the higher end of Boise breakfast, with Greek salads, eggs benedict, and BLT's. It's worth eating there at any time of day, particularly their burgers. Locavore is also very attentive to any dietary restrictions.

Loud, raucous, and oversized, Big City Coffee is nothing if not festive. Serving breakfast and lunch all day, every day, Big City Coffee is one of the favorite spots for Boiseans despite its unusual location. It's a few blocks west of the Grove, surrounded by picture framing stores and auto-mechanics. Stupidly large portions; their motto is "bigger is better" and they mean it.. Big City has options for gluten free for both their sandwiches and baked goods, so be sure to check out what's been made fresh that day.

Goldy's Breakfast Bistro: if you try and to go to Goldy's without a reservation on Sunday you are going to be sorry. The most popular breakfast place in Boise has defended its title well with delicious entrees and a reverence for breakfast staples.

13. LUNCH SPOTS

Local favorite Pie Hole on 8th street serves a greasy slice at the right price. It's actually the cheapest pizza you can find in town, and it also happens to be the best. The staff like to experiment with flavors, combinations like potato bacon, mushroom alfredo; I think I had one with M&M's once. There's a new one all the time. Pie Hole is a favorite stop for college kids and drunken clubbers, but during the day is an inviting place for a bite on their outdoor patio.

Shige's Steakhouse is right across the street from Pie Hole is a bit of a hidden gem. Purveyors of the finest Japanese food in town (better than you'd expect to find in Idaho) and partnered with Ramen Sho next door and the conveyor belt sushi on the other side, Shige's represents variability of price but consistently great quality.

Meraki Greek Street Food, on 8th and Front Street, has satisfying classics like souvlaki and gyros for cheap. Like all good street food shops, they prioritize quality ingredients and fast service.

14.   HAPPY HOUR

The right happy hour can be a bit tough to find in Boise—if you don't know the city. Sometimes it seems like the town goes to sleep at around four p.m., especially in the summertime when the afternoon heat is at its peak. But the people have adapted to survive the harsh conditions, and if you know where to look, an awning and a cocktail are not too far off.

I'm going to start out with the best one. As far as I know, The Reef has the best happy hour on the planet. Absolutely unbelievable deals and top quality fare, the Reef is a place to take large parties if you need somewhere with some space. Bring along a backpack for all the leftovers.

The Matador on 8th Street serves classic tapas: a thousand tiny plates. Make sure you're stopping here for a snack because the numerous tantalizing Spanish features can easily grab your attention.

Bittercreek Alehouse's late night happy hour can save you. I have been on the edge of defeat as I've stumbled into Bittercreek Alehouse, when almost everywhere else in Boise had closed their kitchen. The Alehouse is already home to fantastic burgers, and their diverse happy hour menu can provide a hearty meal and some solid brews late in the night.

Red Feather Lounge features warm and comfortable fare in a tasteful lounge. Neighbored with Bittercreek, be sure to investigate Red Feather if you crave a soft evening with some superb wines; the bartenders at Red Feather are excellent. It's also a lovely spot for Sunday brunch.

15. SNACKS AND SWEETS

Boise has no shortage of snack bars, sweet shops, and quick stops for some delicious fast food.

Cravin's Sweet Shop (formerly Powells'): A novelty candy shop selling old-fashioned and hard to find classics, as well as sodas, gelato, and cotton candy.

Bar Guernica: not your typical pub food. It's a Basque bar in downtown Boise featuring traditional Basque fare and delicious laid-back soul food. Worth a visit for those interested in the multicultural side of Boise, and for those who really crave some good lamb.

Goody's: The number one sweet shop in Boise, Goody's is an institution. Situated in the North End right by Camel's Back Park, Goody's has been making and serving their own candy and ice cream for decades. When you enter you feel a keen longing for a malt and two straws.

Westside Drive-In: Hands down the best milkshake place in Boise, although there is an ongoing feud with the heretics who believe the title goes to Fanci Freez. It's all a matter of preference; Westside has dozens of flavors and will make custom ones for you, even doing their best to invent one on the spot. They moved locations to Southeast Boise in 2011 to accommodate demand, and have been featured on Diners, Drive-In's, and Dives. A must visit for any milkshake aficionado.

Fanci Freez: The second best milkshake place in the city is also a hot spot for a cone. Located just off State Street and 14th, it may be as old as ice cream itself.

16. PLACES FOR DINNER

A casual dinner is not hard to find in Boise, as most Idahoans prefer to play it cool when they go out. Most establishments downtown are open until 11 p.m., and most in the surrounding neighborhoods at least until 10 p.m.. Boise now has more selection than ever, so if you want Vietnamese, Thai, Chinese, Spanish, or Italian, you'll find all of those downtown.

Chicago Pizza Connection: Normally an unnoteworthy chain, this one has been around for decades in an old, yellow adobe building with trellis vines and a patio. It's a good place for a casual Italian fare with family and friends and a menu independent from the chain.

10 Barrel Brewing: A favorite of mine for their unique burgers and outstanding brews. Usually packed but hardly ever a wait, 10 Barrel is a solid choice for some American-style burgers and sandwiches, as well as pizza, pasta, and salad.

Yen-Ching Restaurant: I never gave this place a second glance until my friend hired them to cater a party. Wow. This place is totally underrated, and anyone who's eaten there knows why this nondescript restaurant is still in business after 30 years. Yen-Ching serves Chinese food staples on 9th Street for cheap.

Flatbread Neapolitan Pizza: Some of the best pizza anywhere for the best prices, Flatbread specializes in Neapolitan pizza, the hot-stone oven, thin-crust style. Their flavor combinations are dazzling and original, their wines are delicious, and their two locations are convenient and inviting.

17. FINE DINING

If you want a step above casual, Boise is furnished with a number of upscale to high-end restaurants, most of which would require a reservation on a Friday or Saturday night.

Fork: One of the most interesting and successful restaurants in Boise, Fork was the first restaurant in Idaho to emphasize farm-to-table cooking and locally sourced ingredients. You should always make a reservation for dinner there because the wait on a weeknight can be 40 minutes to an hour, however it's a must-try for its outstanding entrées and beautiful desserts. Be sure to order the buttercake.

Red Feather is very chic, very tasteful dining. The portions are not large, but are takes on American comfort-food: rich, filling, and delectable. The drinks are outstanding and the place is bustling most nights with lively energy, so be sure to make a reservation here too.

For classic Italian with a sparkling veneer, Alavita is the polished sister of Fork, where squid ink pasta and bruschetta are served with the same farm-to-table philosophy. It's the kind of place where a collared shirt is recommended but you could furtively unbutton your pants if you ate too many ravioli. I've had the privilege of eating there only once and it was unforgettable: bruschetta followed by minty lamb rigatoni, ending with tiramisu.

Camel's Crossing is somewhat of a secret in Boise. Located in the North End, people have been gushing about the perfectly assembled plates and the attention to detail. The fare is homey and accessible, but their nuanced combinations of flavors are striking. The 4-course meal on the dinner menu is an exceptional value, so keep an eye on the Sunchoke Panna Cotta for dessert. Go for happy hour if you're in the neighborhood.

18. BARS AND PUBS

A good bar is easy to find in Boise. Aside from the ones already mentioned for their happy hours, some are worth a visit for their unique flair or ludicrously cheap shots. Cactus Bar is one of those places. It's hailed as the best dive bar in town where "every hour is happy hour," and they mean it. With round-the-clock bargain well drinks and suspiciously cheap beers, you can be certain to get your buzz on alarmingly quickly for next to nothing—and, if it's game day, you can just let the crowd wash you into the stadium down the road.

For the nerds and the nostalgic, Space Bar is the place. The website depicts the owner grinning in a Star Trek shirt against a nebulous purple background. When it opened in 2014, Space Bar attracted a great deal of attention from the local press: home to about

20 arcade games and dozens of board games, it was lauded as a mecca for Generations X and Y, the first place of it's kind in Boise to create the atmosphere of digital booziness already popular in Portland and Seattle. It's a sweet space, great during foul weather, and sure to dazzle with its glittering lights and soft beeps and boops. Good beers too.

Finally, my favorite spot for a casual drink is the Press and Pony, a cozy and inviting space where the bartenders will converse warmly and fix you a specialty cocktail they think you'll enjoy. It's a nice place if you want to drink alone or with one other.

19. GET LOOSE

Maybe it's time to leave the kids at home. If you need a night to let loose, 8th street is where you want to be: the site of numerous bars and a smattering of clubs up and down, this thoroughfare is jam-packed at Friday and Saturday nights. Check out Fatty's for a younger crowd in their 20's and 30's, and the Balcony, the premier LGBTQ bar of Boise for groups of all ages. Be sure to catch the raucous drag shows there every Monday night. If it's a weeknight, you might consider catching a comedy show at Liquid Lounge.

20. STAYING SAFE

Safety in Boise is different from bigger cities. There's a slim chance of theft in the city, but avoid interacting with belligerent people particularly in bars and at sporting events. Use common sense and leave the area if you sense trouble and avoid engaging anyone intoxicated.

21. LAST CALL

Boise may not be a conservative place, but Idaho is. You won't find any liquor in grocery stores, and Liquor stores are run by the state and close at 10 p.m. sharp. The bars close at 2 a.m. citywide. Make sure you know when the bars close so that you don't miss out on a late night meal or get started too late at night.

22. SECRET GEMS

The actual best milkshake in Boise is at Merrit's Cafe way up State Street. Merrit's used to be a 24-

hour diner servicing truckers and wanderers, but is now only open until 2 a.m.. Owned by George Merrit, a horse racer and local philanthropist, it's the source of the best decaf and legitimately an amazing milkshake, but is also famous for their scones (which are more like dutch babies), which come slathered in berry compote or cinnamon sugar.

Another special spot in town is The Flicks, an independent theater that still manages to sell and rent movies for way under normal prices. Not only that, they serve a wide selection of beer and wine, curated snack foods, and small little entrée items. The Flicks honors the spirit of the movies more than any other theater I know, offering unique films and low prices just because they can. They've stayed secret partially because of their odd location, tucked behind the Inn at 500 Capitol on a one-way street. It's perfect for a rainy day or a summer evening.

The Flying M Cafe is not really a secret; it's considered by many to be the best coffee shop in town due to its charming decor and relaxing atmosphere, but many tourists pass-by without ever visiting. It can be difficult to find a table at times, but outdoor seating and a diverting gift shop make up for the time lost while waiting, and honestly the wait is rarely more than 5 minutes. The Flying M is on the corner of 6th and Idaho. Guido's Pizza, a great New York-style joint, is right around the side.

23.   FREAK ALLEY

There's nowhere that represents the personality of Boise like Freak Alley. When local artists came together to beautify a downtown parking garage, community admiration brought their works out onto all the blank walls between 7th and 9th. Starting in the garage next to Saint-Lawrence Gridiron (good smoked meats) are the oldest murals, the ones that have been there since 2006-2007. Going up and out into the alleyway between Bannock Street and Idaho Street, you'll find an ever-shifting array of paintings all the way to 9th Street. They're not meant solely for public satisfaction: many haunting murals and urgent messages dots the walls alongside the whimsical and the strange.

24.   SHOPPING DOWNTOWN

Downtown Boise has always had a charming array of boutiques, shops, and gift stores, but it wasn't until recently that there was much variety. In the last ten years, and particularly the last five, Boise has seen so much growth that new condos, hotels, and high-rises arc going up downtown. There is much to see and do in the city center, but not so much that you need more than a day or two. I recommend checking out Capitol Boulevard, 8th Street, Idaho Street, and in particular The Record Exchange, The Flying M Cafe, Rediscovered Books, and Taters.

25. WHEN TO VISIT

Summer is generally the best time of year to visit Boise because most Boiseans are out in droves with the sun. Most of the festivals, events, and outdoor activities take place during the months of July and August into early September. That being said, the months of May and September, when the heat has lessened, are absolutely perfect. The weather is ideal during this time. August in Boise can be unbearably hot, consistently climbing above 100 °F for several days in a row. June and July are more bearable, and higher temperatures usually mean an opportunity to raft the Boise River, grab ice cream, or head up the mountains into the alpine air. There's always ways to beat the heat.

It's also important to know that because Boise is a technically a desert, the low humidity means that it cools down quickly at night. Summer evenings are always pleasant after 7 or 8 pm, and the warm air makes outdoor activities enjoyable until 1 or 2 in the morning, but watch out for a sharp dip in temperature after 2 a.m.!

If you are a fan of winter sports and activities, Boise transforms in late November. The first snows usually fall in the mountains by this time, and oftentimes in town, as well. If not, it almost always snows before January. You'll see holiday lights across the hillsides and snowmen decorating parks and neighborhood streets, decorations strung up in store windows and across the boulevards downtown.

26. SKIING NEAR THE CITY

If it's snowing or raining, that means it's snowing up in the mountains. Idaho is home to at least half a dozen great ski hills scattered around the state. They range anywhere from shoestring, where the runs may not be open for lack of snow, to designer, where they'll make snow if they need it. Bogus Basin is the best place to start as the ideal synthesis of value and quality. Bogus Basin Mountain was purchased by local magnate J.R. Simplot for millions back in 1942, but he turned around and traded it to the city of Boise for one penny, fulfilling the wishes of every skier in Boise for an affordable, nearby hill. Located only 45 minutes from downtown, Bogus Basin is a step out of the bustle of city life into the bustlier festivity of winter sports. Depending on the snowfall, there could be hundreds to thousands of people on the slopes, but the secret to skipping the lines lies in heading up really early or pretty late, or going on a weekday, or both. And some days the weather is beautiful, sunny, bright, and brilliant and there are just no lines for the lifts. The runs are kept in great shape, their quality generally depending more on the kind of snowfall than the maintenance of the hill crew. The back of the mountain is accessible by trails and has its own lifts and runs suitable for more advanced skiers, while the front is usually more populated. Keep an eye out for countless renovations occurring between 2017 and 2020; the hill is still open, but they plan on making improvements to just about every feature of the park to improve customer experience and better reflect Boise's growing significance as a center of outdoor sports.

27. SKIING OUT-OF-THE-WAY

Other hills to consider are Brundage, Tamarack, and Sun Valley, all of which are highly regarded internationally but come with a higher price tag. Sun Valley and Tamarack in particular are pristine resorts nestled in beautiful and temperate mountains where many American presidents have come to ski. If choosing one of these resorts, have your room at its respective lodge picked out far in advance, as demand can be startlingly high in wintertime. Both resorts are worth visiting in the summertime, as well.

Brundage is somewhat less accessible than Tamarack or Sun Valley, being located 3 hours north of Boise in McCall, and is therefore less busy and less expensive, but in my opinion is a match for Sun Valley in the quality of its runs and infrastructure.

For those looking to travel even further off the beaten track, Anthony Lakes in East Idaho is absolutely dirt cheap; Soldier Mountain and Grand Targhee are virtually unknown outside of Idaho, and feature dozens of named runs and significant annual snowfall. For more options and details, check Other References at the end.

28. SNOW DAY

If it's been snowing all day and skiing is not your style, you still have options. One of the most beloved past-times of Boiseans is heading to Simplot Hill, where the house of J.R. Simplot, patron of Bogus Basin, sits at the top. Nowadays it's the governor's mansion, but the sledding that happens on the slopes of the giant hill is such an entrenched tradition that no one noticed the change. Some sleds can be bought at Greenwood's across the street, but beware: both Greenwood's and the hill can be crowded on snowy weekends.

The same is true of the beloved tubing hill that's also at Bogus Basin. They serve on reservation basis, so if you're going to spend the day up there it's best to plan ahead. The tubing hill at Bogus rivals the slopes themselves for popularity. The 100 yard hill is an absolute riot, especially because of a moving mat on the side that carries you back up once you reach the bottom. But a secret only the locals know is that the tube hill is actually worse if it's snowed recently; it benefits most from frequent snowfalls and some time for it to be packed down into ice.

29. WINTER WANDERING

One of my favorite ways to pass a relaxing winter day is to head to some particular parks in the city. Camel's Back Park in the North End (the one near the famous candy store, Goody's) is dazzling under a fresh coat of snow. The big sandy hill becomes a big white mound, and it doesn't take long for hordes of kids to take every scrap of snow in the park and pile it up or hurl it at one another. It's great. Ann Morrison and Julia Davis are dazzling just for their size.

One particularly special event in Boise is the Winter Gardens-a-Glow, hosted by the Botanical Gardens of Boise near the old penitentiary. Every year, volunteers string up millions of lights across the trees and flowers, adding more and more lights annually. If that at first sounds a bit banal, I cannot stress enough how truly beautiful the display is. The event evokes the spirit of the holidays more than anywhere else in the city, and people of all ages come out in droves every night to stroll the gardens sipping complimentary hot chocolate and cider. If you're looking to pass a romantic evening with someone or to absolutely blow your kids' minds, then you absolutely ought to check it out. A must see, on from late November to New Year's Day.

30. INVERSIONS

Sometimes during the winter, Boise gets an unpleasant weather pattern called an "inversion." When pollution gets trapped in the valley under a blanket of falling cold air, it has a tendency to stay there for days or even a couple weeks. The air quality is particularly bad if it hasn't snowed or rained for a while, another reason the people of Boise worship precipitation of any kind. It's important to note that it isn't harmful to your health unless you have serious asthma or another breathing condition, and that you can escape to the mountains or forest easily if you need a breath of fresh air.

31. INDOOR ACTIVITIES

One of my favorite spots in Boise to pass the day indoors is a bowling alley called Westy's Garden Lanes. It has all the classic vibes of an old bowling alley without the haze of cigarette smoke. Oddly, they serve the best french fries in Boise, probably because they've had about 30 years to perfect them, so make sure to grab a large order and burger besides. It's easy to spend several hours there because the lanes are cheap, the food is good, there's never a wait, and the

43

building has billiards and some arcade games in case you get bored. Typical American bowling at its very best.

Sometimes a night at the bars or galavanting across the wilderness is just too much work. For those looking for a fresh way to pass the time inside, consider ABU Games on Cole Road near Edwards 21. ABU Games sells tabletop games of every kind, from your basic Monopoly and Settlers of Catan all the way to escapades of eldritch horror and civilization building. The game store is friendly with customers looking to explore what's for sale, offering practically every board game in the house to be played for free on-site. Having done this myself, I can recommend their selection: with more than 50 table top games to try, it's easy to spend an afternoon here. It can be a bit hard to locate, so use Google to send you to the right spot, and treat yourself to a bit of lunch at the Chef's Hut nearby if you're there in the morning!

32. PLACES TO TAKE A WALK

At any time of year, a nice stroll through a garden or park can be the perfect way to introduce yourself to the town. The Rose Gardens in Julia Davis Park are serene in the spring and summer when the buds have bloomed, and The Botanical Gardens are expansive and well-tended. Warm Springs Boulevard and Harrison Boulevard in the North End both feature surprisingly grandiose homes, shrouded in leafy foliage in the summer and bedecked with Christmas decorations in the winter.

The Village at Meridian has a quaint and posh outdoor mall that's either lavishly decorated in winter or a refuge from the heat in the summer. The Village is equipped with a superb cinema and this funny fountain that does Vegas-style rock concerts on the hour. Those looking for a stroll and some shopping might consider making the trip out to Eagle, thirty minutes from downtown.

33. THE GREENBELT AND THE RIVERSIDE

If you are looking for some peace and quiet, the Greenbelt that runs along the Boise River through practically the entire town is picturesque, with drooping cottonwoods and wildlife teeming in every corner. A popular place for naturalists, bird-watchers, cyclists, and folks walking their dogs, the Greenbelt feels both isolated from the city and comfortable, with its wide trails and many benches. There are sections that are paved for bikes, and parts that are unpaved dirt for walkers, but pedestrians are welcome to stroll along the paved lengths in town provided they are cautious of the cyclists who run the show. If you decide to take a walk along its lengths, keep an eye out for beaches and little islands to while away time stacking stones and playing in the sand, or pack a picnic to eat on a log by the water. Just make sure to leave no trace and pick up after yourself.

Specific sections for walkers are down by Bown Crossing near the Parkcenter Bridge, where bicycles are expressly prohibited. The dirt path leads for several miles to the Southeast in one direction, and connects back to the paved portion heading west. This is a particularly good spot to spot wildlife like ferrets, hawks, beavers, and especially the Great Blue Herons who build their ludicrously large nests in the tops of nearby cottonwood trees.

34. HIKING AND BIKING

The outdoors are the best of what Idaho has to offer. Be sure to investigate the kinds of places you want to see, whether that's mountains or forests, in-town or outside of it. There are far too many options to list here, so I'm only going to list those nearest town.

Behind the Old Idaho Penitentiary is the trailhead to Table Rock, the site of the big glowing cross and the best view of Boise. The trail criss-crosses the hillside, leading off into miles of side trails to other mesas. The walk up to Tablerock is an easy one, only thirty minutes with a steep few feet near the end. Conversely, it's also possible to drive up the backside if you just want the view.

Bogus Basin is not just a winter resort. In fact, the board of investors is trying with all their might to increase summer attendance to the slopes, where scenic hiking and biking abound. They plan to renovate a number of the amenities in 2017 and 2018, adding an "alpine coaster" (picture a slide with a wheeled sled), a ropes course, an "aerial adventure course," and more. It all looks pretty promising. The air is cool in the summertime due to the elevation, and shady trees make it a place to escape the heat.

For those looking for some quick exercise, the Veterans Reserve is more of giant park that eventually kind of blends with the wild foothills. It's dog and bike friendly, and loops around for five, ten, and fifteen mile circuits along the crests and gullies of hills. It's a lovely spot, but hardly shaded in the summertime, so head there in the morning before the heat sends you packing.

This one is a secret one. In the fall and winter, no-name islands in the Boise River sometimes become accessible for a short period of time. These sanctuaries can be quite large, but due to the rising waters in spring and summer are virtually unknown. It's the place for those who like serene walks near river wildlife, and those who like exploring undiscovered places for treasures. These islands attract all kinds of people.

35. FOOTBALL

Boise tends to go a bit wild for football games. The favorite local team is actually a college one, the Boise State Broncos, who have had success in the recent past in bowl games and championships. Football fans would find it worthwhile to catch a Boise Broncos game in the fall and winter. The team is nationally renowned, known for their stunning tricks plays and dramatic upsets, and Boiseans are proud to be home to such a popular team. Catching a game at Bronco Stadium is one of the most festive experiences Boise has to offer. Crowds of tailgaters fill the parking lots and the bars overflow with revelers in orange and blue, all poised to converge on the Smurf Turf, Boise's blue astroturf field.

36. WATER SPORTS

Idaho is famous for its watersports. Kayaking, boating, and rafting are all within the city or nearby, whether that's a day at Lucky Peak Reservoir or a cool afternoon on the Boise River. Boise River Raft and Tube Rentals is located at the push-off point for rafters in Barber Park, and you can find paddleboards and kayaks at Idaho River Sports downtown. Boats might require a little more effort, but a good place to start is Boise Outdoor Toy Share, where locals let others use their outdoor equipment for a daily fee. You'll have to visit their location on 8th and Myrtle to see what's available.

37. RAFTING THE BOISE RIVER

Every year, starting mostly in mid June but picking up speed in July and August, amatuer rafters flood the Boise River with their coolers and squirt guns. They pile in at Barber Park in the morning and afternoon for the two or three hour journey to Ann Morrison Park in the city center. This tradition is so old that there is city-sponsored infrastructure in place to make it possible for anyone to participate, including a bus that travels between the parks carrying rafters from their cars to the push-off points, and compressed air nearby to fill your raft. Also at Barber Park is a rental office for tubes, rafts, lifejackets, and patch kits, catering to any need for a fair price. If visiting in the summer and feeling adventurous, a day rafting the river is an excellent way to beat the heat and feel the spirit of the city. Just remember not to bring any electronics or valuables unless they're triple-sealed in ziploc bags, and not to litter in the river.

38. CAMPING

Oh, how I could go on. If you're lucky enough to have a few extra days and an explorer's excitement; if you have a car, truck, or RV; if you can't stand this concrete jungle any longer and you just want to see some unspoiled wilderness, you have come to the right state. I have been to all of these locations personally and can attest to their serene bliss and piney aromas. Those without gear can rent the necessary equipment from REI (just remember that an REI membership makes it much cheaper), or Boise State University, which has some real solid rates. I can really only tell you the general idea of each place because to attempt to explain the pros and cons of every campsite in Idaho is it's own book—several, in fact—so here are my favorites with just a little extra information.

Mack's Creek: Just 20 minutes from town at Lucky Peak reservoir. Great facilities and good for rock climbers.

Ten Mile Campground: Convenience only an hour from downtown.

French Creek: Near civilization and nestled in the heart of the woods of Lake Cascade.

Bruno Sand Dunes: Superior stargazing and a unique and dreamy terrain.

Kirkham Campground (home of the world-class Kirkham Hot Springs): a skip from multiple nearby hot springs and a couple whitewater rafting companies.

Stanley/Challis: Also near a rafting company (my favorite, The Payette River Company)

Lewiston: Forested glades at elevation. Scenic river cliffs.

Alturas Lake: Calm and beautiful lake in East Idaho for fishing and kayaking. Unparalleled stargazing.

Succor Creek and Leslie Gulch: Some of the best hiking in the country nearby at Leslie Gulch. Succor Creek is wonderful on its own.

More information about campsites is available in the Other Resources section.

39. STARGAZING

Idaho is unique in America for being home to the first ever Dark Sky Reserve. This is an area of land designated by the federal government to be below a certain threshold for light pollution every year. The Central Idaho Dark Sky Reserve is near the Sawtooth National Recreation Area, both protected parks, making Idaho Dark Sky one of the best places in the country to see the undiluted brilliance of the night sky. Having camped all over Idaho and inside the reserve, I can attest to its magnificence: I have never seen more stars and planets anywhere else—and I've been to the Sahara. Visiting the reserve and staying for a night is an unforgettable experience, particularly for those with of a telescope.

Other great places to see the night sky include Bruneau Sand Dunes, a mere 45 minutes from Boise, and Lowman, Idaho, which is farther than the reserve. Bruneau is special for its observatory, which on summer nights frequently opens its doors to stargazers wishing to see the planets up close. Lowman is notable for being a very small town with a few more amenities than either of the parks, such as lodging and grocery.

40. WILDLIFE YOU OUGHT TO KNOW ABOUT

Idaho is home to beasts of all shapes and sizes, and if you want to keep some distance between them and yourself, then you ought to know about where they roam. The most important rule when entering the wilderness is, when you're not using it, hide your food. Animals aren't interested in you, not even the big ones; they only want to eat that Snickers in your back pocket. Keeping your food in your car (or tied up in a tree when camping) will help you avoid attracting unwanted attention. Bears, mountain lions, wolves, coyotes, badgers, and wolverines all populate the Idaho wilderness, as well as animals like deer, raccoons, eagles, and snakes. The former will seek you out if they smell food, and the latter will primarily avoid interaction with humans. Remember to be aware of your surroundings and the kinds of animals that live there!

Black bears and brown bears in Idaho are generally shy around humans, but can be unafraid and extremely clever at finding food. When camping, leave food in your car or high up in the trees where they can't reach it. For the most part, bears are skittish and can be frightened off with loud noises (unless they think their cub is in danger) so if you cross paths with a bear, don't run from it. Instead, back away slowly while keeping your eyes on it. Raccoons will almost always avoid a confrontation but can give you grief if your supplies are left out.

In the high plains above the city are mountain lions and coyotes. Both are generally smart enough to avoid interactions with humans, but if you see a mountain lion then its best to leave the area. If you're near town, call 911 and let them know.

Both in the plains and the foothills are snakes of all kinds, including rattlesnakes. I can tell you from personal experience that it takes more than you might think for a rattlesnake to bite you, but if you hear that characteristic rattle, best turn around and walk back the way you came. A rattlesnake bite far from transportation can easily be fatal, particularly if you're out of cell service. Staying on the trail will help avoid an encounter.

For more information check the Other Resources at the end.

41. GET WEST

Idaho is home to some particularly Western charms, not the least of which are the Western Idaho Fair and the Snake River Stampede.

The Snake River Stampede is one of the ten largest seasonal rodeos in the country, taking place in mid July for about four days. It's just about the most iconic rodeo experience you could ask for, with bow-legged cowpokes moseying this way and that, and rodeo clowns in the rings. The organizers hold dozens of events, from bronco-riding to cattle-rustling to bullfighting (but not the Spanish kind), to even a contest for Miss Rodeo Queen. Participation is encouraged for certain events, in particular "mutton busting," a children's rodeo ride on sheep-back, or for the concert that takes place Friday night. It's as "country" as you can get.

The Western Idaho Fair arrives in August and is like most others except for the variety of animal auctions taking place behind the scenes. Most of the ranchers and farmers near Boise actually use the fair to buy, sell, and trade animals, and a number of rare breeds and prize-winning beasts are on display like Scottish Highland Cows and a ludicrous number of horses and donkeys. Two large tents are erected as petting zoos and two even larger warehouses are filled with small animals of all kinds, with the larger ones occupying the stables in the back.

42. DAY TRIPS

Boise is surrounded by strange and curious attractions that will pique the imagination and create lasting memories. All of them involve a certain degree of outdoorsmanship, as the infrastructure outside of Boise have remained mostly unchanged since the 1960's.

Craters of the Moon and Shoshone Ice Caves is one of the most unusual places anywhere in America and perhaps the world. A blasted landscape of volcanic rock, Craters of the Moon was used to train American astronauts in the 1960's because of its considerable resemblance to the surface of the moon. Don't worry about getting around; a paved walking trail winds through the park. While you're there, keep an eye out for signs to the Shoshone Ice Cave, a perpetually frozen labyrinth of ice that winds through dormant lava tubes. Tours with experienced guides go into the ice caves with lanterns on a metal walkway, but you can still stick your hand out and feel the slick walls as you move deeper inside. Beware that at some point they may turn out the lights so you can experience the dark.

For a more fanciful and familiar outing, consider Idaho City. Nestled up in the mountains about an hour from Boise, the old mining city was nearly abandoned 150 years ago when the gold dried up, but the 100 residents who remained managed to keep the town on the map. Now it's a booming town of 500 people where Boiseans go to find incredible ice cream and see a place that still features most of its Old West architecture.

43. HOT SPRINGS

Idaho has more hot springs than any other state in the nation, and significantly more that are reachable and usable. One of the most famous hot springs of the Mountain West, Kirkham Hot Springs overlooks the South fork of the Payette River. It's popular because of the way that natural minerals in the water have over many years deposited themselves as rims of giant stone pools. The piping hot mineral water pours over the edges into others until each is a slightly different temperature from the last. Native Idahoans have a tradition of working their way up to the hottest pools and then jumping into the Payette river, which eddies in a natural swirl near the springs. Lots of parking is nearby (bring $5 in cash for parking) and food is allowed provided people pick up after themselves. Close to Stanley and it's campgrounds and the hot springs resort in Challis, the Kirkham Hot Springs are the freeish option where mingling with the natives is a guarantee. For bonus points, go in the winter while its snowing and enjoy the feeling of snowflakes falling on your face as you relax in a 110 °F/ 44 °C tub.

Not all of the hot springs in Idaho are scattered around the wilderness. Challis hot springs is one of the most geologically active areas in the state, and among the many public hot springs is the Challis Hot Springs Resort. Though they once offered a Bed and Breakfast, the Challis Hot Springs Resort still offers the most developed hot springs outside of Boise, where two pools—one larger and 100 °F, and one smaller at 105 °F—are fed through their gravel beds by piping hot mineral water. You can generally expect a private day spent there as attendance is usually low at all times of the year, ensuring a relaxing and restorative outing from Boise or your campground nearby.

This last one is the most unique: Boat Box Hot Springs is just basically a kettle for you to cook in. A recycled mining shovel was turned into a tub with water flowing in through an attached pipe stuck into the hillside. It's a cozy spot; more than three people are going to be a bit crowded, and I recommend going on a weekday to minimize your chances of sharing. Oh, and you'll have to scoop river water into it to make it bearable, but there's a bucket there already.

44. WORLD CENTER FOR BIRDS OF PREY

It had to be somewhere! The World Center for Birds of Prey has a humble title, but it's one of the foremost habitat and species recovery centers in the world. In 2010, an international celebration was held there to commemorate the removal of the Peregrine Falcon from the endangered species list, a feat in which the Birds of Prey Center played an integral part. Visiting here can easily take up a whole day. Walking through the many acres of trails and sanctuaries, exploring the falconry museum, seeing a live demonstration or interacting with the hands-on exhibits all impart the tenderness of the Center's mission: to introduce people to some magnificent animals and encourage them to protect their habitats. It's close to town, on the side of the city most people never visit. It's worth going just to see the California Condors and the birds wheeling over the plains.

45. FAMILY FUN

If you and the kids want to get out and catch some sun then there's no better place than Roaring Springs Water Park. Recently synthesized with its neighbor, Wahooz, the pair are an easy place to beat the heat. There's endless diversion for kids, and adults can relax in some of the sheltered islands under the beach umbrellas peppering the park, or loop endlessly on the Lazy River.

Jump Time downtown is another hot spot for families, particularly for parents who don't mind a bit of bouncing. Jump Time keeps chaperones on staff (college kids bouncing apathetically) so you can stroll around Julia Davis District.

Alternatively, a lazy Sunday could be spent at the Train Depot downtown, which showcases the city's industrial and locomotive history amidst a charming park. Nearby is also the Boise Art Museum, which recently expanded its collections.

The Boise Zoo, located in Julia Davis Park, is more substantial than anyone would suspect, given that Boise is not a large city. A unique feature is the Butterfly Walkthrough that starts in May and goes through the summertime. Giant butterflies flap around your head and land on your clothes, maybe your face. The city adores the zoo and attendance in the summertime is overwhelming, such that the Boise Zoo Foundation has been able to renovate once every eight or nine years for the last thirty years. An ongoing expansion to the Africa exhibit has nearly half the Zoo closed until the summer of 2019, but new animals will be in arriving including crocodiles, African wild dogs, vervet monkeys and otters.

46. JAIALDI

Every five years, Boise is home to a fabulous festival called Jaialdi (pronounced Hi-al-dee) from July 28th to August 2nd, a celebration of the Basque Diaspora and their community in Boise. All kinds of delicious delicacies like elotes, paella, and esquites line the streets and dances and parades and music fill the air until late in the night. The next festival is in 2020, and concurrent festivals will be held every five years after, the biggest happening every 25 years. I was lucky enough to attend a 25th Jaialdi in 2010 when hundreds of Basque came from all over the world to celebrate with the Boise community, and it was the craziest party I'd ever seen. Bardenay Bar and Grill cleared their tables and chairs to make room for the nearly one hundred people crammed in, elbows locked as they hollered Basque folk music and drank flagons of beer.

47. SPIRIT OF BOISE BALLOON CLASSIC

Many people who've lived in the Northwest associate Boise with hot-air balloons. The city has been home to an ongoing hot-air balloon festival for decades, the Spirit of Boise Balloon Classic. It used to be that you could take longer rides in the hot-air balloons. Nowadays only tethered ups-and-downs are allowed, but that shouldn't stop you from checking it out if you can get there by 6:45 or 7 a.m.. Watching the dozens of huge, colorful balloons take off into the dawn is an unforgettable experience. There are some things to know before going, and they are: dress warm, don't bring your pets, and don't touch the balloons.

48. TREEFORT

Treefort is a budding music festival in downtown Boise that as of 2019 is entering its eighth year. Because Boise is a walking city with a tightly-knit urban center, the festival is sprawled among city landmarks like the JUMP and Capitol Park. Since its inception, Treefort has expanded into a multi-faceted, multi-venue four day festival including (but not limited to) Alefort, Comedyfort, Yogafort, Kidfort, Hackfort, and more, and with artists from all over the country headlining and new Idaho artists making their debut, Treefort is attracting national attention. It's one of the premiere yearly events in Idaho, and in 2015, Treefort was noted by the City of Boise's Cultural Ambassador "for being an event that genuinely reflects the energy across mediums that is happening in the Boise community and cultural scene, and for the vision of connecting Boise and its creatives with other communities around the region, the country and around the world." Attendance features visitors and locals of all kinds, and the spirit of the festival emphasizes acceptance and humanity in agreement with the casual friendliness of Boise. Tickets go on sale early September the year before, with choices like Early Bird being the cheapest all the way to the line-skipper's Zipline Pass, the most expensive.

49. ART IN THE PARK AND HYDE PARK STREET FAIR

September is practically the best month to be in Boise. Two major festivals, Art in the Park and the Hyde Park Street Fair, both set up early in the month. Art in the Park is one of the Northwest's premiere cultural festivals, a collection of over 200 artists in Julia Davis Park. Visitors can enjoy live music, a huge selection of food, and thousands of original works.

The Hyde Park Street Fair (at Camel's Back Park) is smaller and crunchier. Tie-dye shirts and hemp hoodies make thoroughfares through Hyde Park and people dressed in costumes of all kinds abound. Get your name written on a grain of rice or buy some stylish blown glass.

50. IDAHO SHAKESPEARE FESTIVAL

Every year the Idaho Shakespeare Company puts on dozens of plays that the people of Boise gobble up. Part of the excitement comes from the talent of the cast and crew, who could and do rival any city in America, but the rest comes from the pleasantness that an evening of outdoor theater in the summertime can bring. The troupe puts on shows from May to September, and they all sell out in just a few days once tickets go on sale on April 1st, so make sure to plan this part far in advance. In rare cases, tickets can be had on short notice when people give up their seats, so call in if you really want to go. Picnicking in the theatre is an old-standing tradition there, so bring food and drink to enjoy and a blanket or two if you have seats on the grass. Chairs are available for a small rental fee, and there's a cafe on sight if you don't feel like bringing your own grub. The Idaho Shakespeare Festival is one of the gems of Boise and all of Idaho, so take a look and see if any of your favorite plays will be making an appearance.

RECAP! WHY GO TO BOISE?

The Activities: It's easy to find something for everyone due to the city's wide selection of outdoor amenities.

The Personality: The people in Boise are kind, friendly, and welcoming.

The Nature: Gorgeous landscapes and pristine wilderness inside the city and out, and dozens of day trips to make.

BONUS BOOK

50 THINGS TO KNOW ABOUT PACKING LIGHT FOR TRAVEL

PACK THE RIGHT WAY EVERY TIME

AUTHOR: MANIDIPA BHATTACHARYYA

Edited by Melanie Howthorne

ABOUT THE AUTHOR

Manidipa Bhattacharyya is a creative writer and editor, with an education in English literature and Linguistics. After working in the IT industry for seven long years she decided to call it quits and follow her heart instead. Manidipa has been ghost writing, editing, proof reading and doing secondary research services for many story tellers and article writers for about three years. She stays in Kolkata, India with her husband and a busy two year old. In her own time Manidipa enjoys travelling, photography and writing flash fiction.

Manidipa believes in travelling light and never carries anything that she couldn't haul herself on a trip. However, travelling with her child changed the scenario. She seemed to carry the entire world with her for the baby on the first two trips. But good sense prevailed and she is again working her way to becoming a light traveler, this time with a kid.

INTRODUCTION

*He who would travel happily
must travel light.*

-Antoine de Saint-Exupéry

Travel takes you to different places from seas and mountains to deserts and much more. In your travels you get to interact with different people and their cultures. You will, however, enjoy the sights and interact positively with these new people even more, if you are travelling light.

When you travel light your mind can be free from worry about your belongings. You do not have to spend precious vacation time waiting for your luggage to arrive after a long flight. There is be no chance of your bags going missing and the best part is that you need not pay a fee for checked baggage.

People who have mastered this art of packing light will root for you to take only one carry-on, wherever you go. However, many people can find it really hard to pack light. More so if you are travelling with children. Differentiating between "must have" and "just in case" items is the starting point. There will be ample shopping avenues at your destination which are just waiting to be explored.

This book will show you 'packing' in a new 'light' – pun intended – and help you to embrace light packing practices for all of your future travels.

Off to packing!

DEDICATION

I dedicate this book to all the travel buffs that I know, who have given me great insights into the contents of their backpacks.

THE RIGHT TRAVEL GEAR

1. CHOOSE YOUR TRAVEL GEAR CAREFULLY

While selecting your travel gear, pick items that are light weight, durable and most importantly, easy to carry. There are cases with wheels so you can drag them along – these are usually on the heavy side because of the trolley. Alternatively a backpack that you can carry comfortably on your back, or even a duffel bag that you can carry easily by hand or sling across your body are also great options. Whatever you choose, one thing to keep in mind is that the luggage itself should not weigh a ton, this will give you the flexibility to bring along one extra pair of shoes if you so desire.

2. CARRY THE MINIMUM NUMBER OF BAGS

Selecting light weight luggage is not everything. You need to restrict the number of bags you carry as well. One carry-on size bag is ideal for light travel. Most carriers allow one cabin baggage plus one purse, handbag or camera bag as long as it slides under the seat in front. So technically, you can carry two items of luggage without checking them in.

3. PACK ONE EXTRA BAG

Always pack one extra empty bag along with your essential items. This could be a very light weight duffel bag or even a sturdy tote bag which takes up minimal space. In the event that you end up buying a lot of souvenirs, you already have a handy bag to stuff all that into and do not have to spend time hunting for an appropriate bag.

I'm very strict with my packing and have everything in its right place. I never change a rule. I hardly use anything in the hotel room. I wheel my own wardrobe in and that's it.

Charlie Watts

CLOTHES & ACCESSORIES

4. PLAN AHEAD

Figure out in advance what you plan to do on your trip. That will help you to pick that one dress you need for the occasion. If you are going to attend a wedding then you have to carry formal wear. If not, you can ditch the gown for something lighter that will be comfortable during long walks or on the beach.

5. WEAR THAT JACKET

Remember that wearing items will not add extra luggage for your air travel. So wear that bulky jacket that you plan to carry for your trip. This saves space and can also help keep you warm during the chilly flight.

6. MIX AND MATCH

Carry clothes that can be interchangeably used to reinvent your look. Find one top that goes well with a couple of pairs of pants or skirts. Use tops, shirts and jackets wisely along with other accessories like a scarf or a stole to create a new look.

7. CHOOSE YOUR FABRIC WISELY

Stuffing clothes in cramped bags definitely takes its toll which results in wrinkles. It is best to carry wrinkle free, synthetic clothes or merino tops. This will eliminate the need for that small iron you usually bring along.

8. DITCH CLOTHES PACK UNDERWEAR

Pack more underwear and socks. These are the things that will give you a fresh feel even if you do not get a chance to wear fresh clothes. Moreover these are easy to wash and can be dried inside the hotel room itself.

9. CHOOSE DARK OVER LIGHT

While picking your clothes choose dark coloured ones. They are easy to colour coordinate and can last longer before needing a wash. Accidental food spills and dirt from the road are less visible on darker clothes.

10. WEAR YOUR JEANS

Take only one pair of Jeans with you, which you should wear on the flight. Remember to pick a pair that can be worn for sightseeing trips and is equally eloquent for dinner. You can add variety by adding light weight cargoes and chinos.

11. CARRY SMART ACCESSORIES

The right accessory can give you a fresh look even with the same old dress. An intelligent neck-piece, a couple of bright scarves, stoles or a sarong can be used in a number of ways to add variety to your clothing. These light weight beauties can double up as a nursing cover, a light blanket, beach wear, a modesty cover for visiting places of worship, and also makes for an enthralling game of peek-a-boo.

12. LEARN TO FOLD YOUR GARMENTS

Seasoned travellers all swear by rolling their clothes for compact and wrinkle free packing. Bundle packing, where you roll the clothes around a central object as if tying it up, is also a popular method of compact and wrinkle free packing. Stacking folded clothes one on top of another is a big no-no as it makes creases extreme and they are difficult to get rid of without ironing.

13. WASH YOUR DIRTY LAUNDRY

One of the ways to avoid carrying loads of clothes is to wash the clothes you carry. At some places you might get to use the laundry services or a Laundromat but if you are in a pinch, best solution is to wash them yourself. If that is the plan then carrying quick drying clothes is highly recommended, which most often also happen to be the wrinkle free variety.

14. LEAVE THOSE TOWELS BEHIND

Regular towels take up a lot of space, are heavy and take ages to dry out. If you are staying at hotels they will provide you with towels anyway. If you are travelling to a remote place, where the availability of towels look doubtful, carry a light weight travel towel of viscose material to do the job.

15. USE A COMPRESSION BAG

Compression bags are getting lots of recommendation now days from regular travellers. These are useful for saving space in your luggage when you have to pack bulky dresses. While packing for the return trip, get help from the hotel staff to arrange a vacuum cleaner.

FOOTWEAR

16. PUT ON YOUR HIKING BOOTS

If you have plans to go hiking or trekking during your trip, you will need those bulky hiking boots. The best way to carry them is to wear them on flight to save space and luggage weight. You can remove the boots once inside and be comfortable in your socks.

17. PICKING THE RIGHT SHOES

Shoes are often the bulkiest items, along with being the dainty if you are a female. They need care and take up a lot of space in your luggage. It is advisable therefore to pick shoes very carefully. If you plan to do a lot of walking and site seeing, then wearing a pair of comfortable walking shoes are a must. For more formal occasions you can carry durable, light weight flats which will not take up much space.

18. STUFF SHOES

If you happen to pack a pair of shoes, ensure you utilize their hollow insides. Tuck small items like rolled up socks or belts to save space. They will also be easy to find.

TOILETRIES

19. STASHING TOILETRIES

Carry only absolute necessities. Airline rules dictate
that for one carry-on bag, liquids and gels must be in
3.4 ounce (100ml) bottles or less, and must be packed
in a one quart zip-lock bag. If you are planning to stay
in a hotel, the basic things will be provided for you.
It's best is to buy the rest from the local market at
your destination.

20. TAKE ALONG TAMPONS

Tampons are a hard to find item in a lot of countries.
Figure out how many you need and pack accordingly.
For longer stays you can buy them online and have
them delivered to where you are staying.

21. GET PAMPERED BEFORE YOU TRAVEL

Some avid travellers suggest getting a pedicure and
manicure just the day before travelling. This not only
gives you a well kept look, you also save the trouble
of packing nail polish. Remember, every little bit of
weight reduced adds up.

ELECTRONICS

22. LUGGING ALONG ELECTRONICS

Electronics have a large role to play in our lives today. Most of us cannot imagine our lives away from our phones, laptops or tablets. However while travelling, one must consider the amount of weight these electronics add to our luggage. Thankfully smart phones come along with all the essentials tools like a camera, email access, picture editing tools and more. They are smart to the point of eliminating the need to carry multiple gadgets. Choose a smart phone that suits all your requirements and travel with the world in your palms or pocket.

23. REDUCE THE NUMBER OF CHARGERS

If you do travel with multiple electronic devices, you will have to bear the additional burden of carrying all their chargers too. Check if a single charger can be used for multiple devices. You might also consider investing in a pocket charger. These small devices support multiple devices while keeping you charged on the go.

24. TRAVEL FRIENDLY APPS

Along with smart phones come numerous apps, which are immensely helpful in our travels. You name it and you have an app for it at hand – take pictures, sharing with friends and family, torch to light dark roads, maps, checking flight/train times, find hotels and many other things. Use these smart alternatives to traditional items like books to eliminate weight and save space.

I get ideas about what's essential when packing my suitcase.

-Diane von Furstenberg

TRAVELLING WITH KIDS

25. BRING ALONG THE STROLLER

Kids might enjoy walking for a while but they soon tire out and a stroller is the just the right thing for them to rest in while you continue your tour. Strollers also double duty as a luggage carrier and shopping bag holder. Remember to pick a light weight, easy to handle brand of stroller. Better yet, find out in advance if you can rent a stroller at your destination.

26. BRING ONLY ENOUGH DIAPERS FOR YOUR TRIP

Diapers take up a lot of space and add to the weight of your luggage. Therefore it is advisable to carry just enough diapers to last through the trip and a few for afterwards, till you buy fresh stock at your destination. Unless of course you are travelling to a really remote area, in which case you have no choice but to carry the load. Otherwise diapers are something you will find pretty easily.

27. TAKE ONLY A COUPLE OF TOYS

Children are easily attracted by new things in their environment. While travelling they will find numerous 'new' objects to scrutinize and play with. Packing just one favorite toy is enough, or if there is no favorite toy leave out all of them in favor of stories or imaginary games.

28. CARRY KID FRIENDLY SNACKS

Create a small snack counter in your bag to store away quick bites for those sudden hunger pangs. Depending on the child's age this could include chocolates, raisins, dry fruits, granola bars or biscuits. Also keep a bottle of water handy for your little one.

These things do not add much weight and can be adjusted in a handbag or knapsack.

29. GAMES TO CARRY

Create some travel specific, imaginary games if you have slightly grown up children, like spot the attractions. Keep a coloring book and colors handy for in-flight or hotel time. Apps on your smart phone can keep the children engaged with cartoons and story books. Older children are often entertained by games available on phones or tablets. This cuts the weight of luggage down while keeping the kids entertained.

30. LET THE KIDS CARRY THEIR LOAD

A good thing is to start early sharing of responsibilities. Let your child pick a bag of his or her choice and pack it themselves. Keep tabs on what they are stuffing in their bags by asking if they will be using that item on the trip. It could start out being just an entertainment bag initially but with growing years they will learn to sort the useful from the superfluous. Children as little as four can maneuver a small trolley suitcase like a pro- their experience in pull along toys credit. If you are worried that you may be pulling it for them, you may want to start with a backpack.

31. DECIDE ON LOCATION FOR CHILDREN TO SLEEP

While on a trip you might not always get a crib at your destination, and carrying one will make life all the more difficult. Instead call ahead to see if there are any cribs or roll out beds for children. You may even put blankets on the floor. Weave them a story about camping and they will gladly sleep without any trouble.

32. GET BABY PRODUCTS DELIVERED AT YOUR DESTINATION

If you are absolutely paranoid about not getting your favourite variety of diaper or brand of baby food, check out online stores like amazon.com for services in your destination city. You can buy things online ahead of your travel and get them delivered to your hotel upon arrival.

33. FEEDING NEEDS OF YOUR INFANTS

If you are travelling with a breastfed infant, you save the trouble of carrying bottles and bottle sanitization kits. For special food, or medications, you may need to call ahead to make sure you have a refrigerator where you are staying.

34. FEEDING NEEDS OF YOUR TODDLER

With the progression from infancy to toddler, their dietary requirements too evolve. You will have to pack some snacks for travelling time. Fresh fruits and vegetables can be purchased at your destination. Most of the cities you travel to in whichever part of the world, will have baby food products and formulas, available at the local drug-store or the supermarket.

35. PICKING CLOTHES FOR YOUR BABY

Contrary to popular belief, babies can do without many changes of clothes. At the most pack 2 outfits per day. Pack mix and match type clothes for your little one as well. Pick things which are comfortable to wear and quick to dry.

36. SELECTING SHOES FOR YOUR BABY

Like outfits, kids can make do with two pairs of comfortable shoes. If you can get some water resistant shoes it will be best. To expedite drying wet shoes, you can stuff newspaper in them then wrap

them with newspaper and leave them to dry
overnight.

37. KEEP ONE CHANGE OF CLOTHES HANDY

Travelling with kids can be tricky. Keep a change of
clothes for the kids and mum handy in your purse or
tote bag. This takes a bit of space in your hand
luggage but comes extremely handy in case there are
any accidents or spills.

38. LEAVE BEHIND BABY ACCESSORIES

Baby accessories like their bed, bath tub, car seat, crib
etc. should be left at home. Many hotels provide a
crib on request, while car seats can be borrowed from
friends or rented. Babies can be given a bath in the
hotel sink or even in the adult bath tub with a little bit
of water. If you bring a few bath toys, they can be
used in the bath, pool, and out of water. They can also
be sanitized easily in the sink.

39. CARRY A SMALL LOAD OF PLASTIC BAGS

With children around there are chances of a number
of soiled clothes and diapers. These plastic bags help
to sort the dirt from the clean inside your big bag.

These are very light weight and come in handy to other carry stuff as well at times.

PACK WITH A PURPOSE

40. PACKING FOR BUSINESS TRIPS

One neutral-colored suit should suffice. It can be paired with different shirts, ties and accessories for different occasions. One pair of black suit pants could be worn with a matching jacket for the office or with a snazzy top for dinner.

41. PACKING FOR A CRUISE

Most cruises have formal dinners, and that formal dress usually takes up a lot of space. However you might find a tuxedo to rent. For women, a short black dress with multiple accessory options will do the trick.

42. PACKING FOR A LONG TRIP OVER DIFFERENT CLIMATES

The secret packing mantra for travel over multiple climates is layering. Layering traps air around your body creating insulation against the cold. The same light t-shirt that is comfortable in a warmer climate can be the innermost layer in a colder climate.

REDUCE SOME MORE WEIGHT

43. LEAVE PRECIOUS THINGS AT HOME

Things that you would hate to lose or get damaged leave them at home. Precious jewelry, expensive gadgets or dresses, could be anything. You will not require these on your trip. Leave them at home and spare the load on your mind.

44. SEND SOUVENIRS BY MAIL

If you have spent all your money on purchasing souvenirs, carrying them back in the same bag that you brought along would be difficult. Either pack everything in another bag and check it in the airport or get everything shipped to your home. Use an international carrier for a secure transit, but this could be more expensive than the checking fees at the airport.

45. AVOID CARRYING BOOKS

Books equal to weight. There are many reading apps which you can download on your smart phone or tab.

Plus there are gadgets like Kindle and Nook that are thinner and lighter alternatives to your regular book.

CHECK, GET, SET, CHECK AGAIN

46. STRATEGIZE BEFORE PACKING

Create a travel list and prepare all that you think you need to carry along. Keep everything on your bed or floor before packing and then think through once again – do I really need that? Any item that meets this question can be avoided. Remove whatever you don't really need and pack the rest.

47. TEST YOUR LUGGAGE

Once you have fully packed for the trip take a test trip with your luggage. Take your bags and go to town for window shopping for an hour. If you enjoy your hour long trip it is good to go, if not, go home and reduce the load some more. Repeat this test till you hit the right weight.

48. ADD A ROLL OF DUCT TAPE

You might wonder why, when this book has been talking about reducing stuff, we're suddenly asking you to pack something totally unusual. This is because when you have limited supplies, duct tape is immensely helpful for small repairs – a broken bag, leaking zip-lock bag, broken sunglasses, you name it and duct tape can fix it, temporarily.

49. LIST OF ESSENTIAL ITEMS

Even though the emphasis is on packing light, there are things which have to be carried for any trip. Here is our list of essentials:

• Passport/Visa or any other ID

• Any other paper work that might be required on a trip like permits, hotel reservation confirmations etc.

• Medicines – all your prescription medicines and emergency kit, especially if you are travelling with children

• Medical or vaccination records

• Money in foreign currency if travelling to a different country

• Tickets- Email or Message them to your phone

50. MAKE THE MOST OF YOUR TRIP

Wherever you are going, whatever you hope to do we encourage you to embrace it whole-heartedly. Take in the scenery, the culture and above all, enjoy your time away from home.

On a long journey even a straw weighs heavy.

-Spanish Proverb

PACKING AND PLANNING TIPS

A Week before Leaving

- Arrange for someone to take care of pets and water plants.

- Stop mail and newspaper.

- Notify Credit Card companies where you are going.

- Change your thermostat settings.

- Car inspected, oil is changed, and tires have the correct pressure.

- Passports and photo identification is up to date.

- Pay bills.

- Copy important items and download travel Apps.

- Start collecting small bills for tips.

Right Before Leaving

- Clean out refrigerator.

- Empty garbage cans.

- Lock windows.

- Make sure you have the proper identification with you.

- Bring cash for tips.

- Remember travel documents.

- Lock door behind you.

- Remember wallet.

- Unplug items in house and pack chargers.

READ OTHER
GREATER THAN A TOURIST
BOOKS

Greater Than a Tourist San Miguel de Allende Guanajuato Mexico:
50 Travel Tips from a Local by Tom Peterson

Greater Than a Tourist – Lake George Area New York USA:
 50 Travel Tips from a Local by Janine Hirschklau

Greater Than a Tourist – Monterey California United States:
50 Travel Tips from a Local by Katie Begley

 Greater Than a Tourist – Chanai Crete Greece:
50 Travel Tips from a Local by Dimitra Papagrigoraki

Greater Than a Tourist – The Garden Route Western Cape Province
South Africa: 50 Travel Tips from a Local by Li-Anne McGregor van
Aardt

Greater Than a Tourist – Sevilla Andalusia Spain:
50 Travel Tips from a Local by Gabi Gazon

Greater Than a Tourist – Kota Bharu Kelantan Malaysia:
50 Travel Tips from a Local by Aditi Shukla

Children's Book: Charlie the Cavalier Travels the World by Lisa
Rusczyk

> TOURIST

Visit Greater Than a Tourist for Free Travel Tips
http://GreaterThanATourist.com

Sign up for the Greater Than a Tourist Newsletter for discount days, new books, and travel information:
http://eepurl.com/cxspyf

Follow us on Facebook for tips, images, and ideas:
https://www.facebook.com/GreaterThanATourist

Follow us on Pinterest for travel tips and ideas:
http://pinterest.com/GreaterThanATourist

Follow us on Instagram for beautiful travel images:
http://Instagram.com/GreaterThanATourist

> TOURIST

Please leave your honest review of this book on Amazon and Goodreads. Please send your feedback to GreaterThanaTourist@gmail.com as we continue to improve the series. We appreciate your positive and constructive feedback. Thank you.

METRIC CONVERSIONS

TEMPERATURE

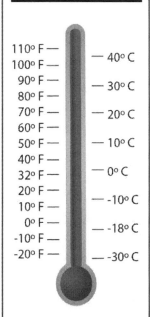

110° F — — 40° C
100° F —
90° F — — 30° C
80° F —
70° F — — 20° C
60° F —
50° F — — 10° C
40° F —
32° F — — 0° C
20° F —
10° F — — -10° C
0° F —
-10° F — — -18° C
-20° F — — -30° C

To convert F to C:

Subtract 32, and then multiply by 5/9 or .5555.

To Convert C to F:

Multiply by 1.8 and then add 32.

32F = 0C

LIQUID VOLUME

To Convert:....................Multiply by
U.S. Gallons to Liters................ 3.8
U.S. Liters to Gallons 26
Imperial Gallons to U.S. Gallons 1.2
Imperial Gallons to Liters....... 4.55
Liters to Imperial Gallons 22
1 Liter = .26 U.S. Gallon
1 U.S. Gallon = 3.8 Liters

DISTANCE

To convert ....Multiply by
Inches to Centimeters 2.54
Centimeters to Inches 39
Feet to Meters....................... .3
Meters to Feet 3.28
Yards to Meters 91
Meters to Yards 1.09
Miles to Kilometers 1.61
Kilometers to Miles............ .62
1 Mile = 1.6 km
1 km = .62 Miles

WEIGHT

1 Ounce = .28 Grams
1 Pound = .4555 Kilograms
1 Gram = .04 Ounce
1 Kilogram = 2.2 Pounds

101

TRAVEL QUESTIONS

- Do you bring presents home to family or friends after a vacation?

- Do you get motion sick?

- Do you have a favorite billboard?

- Do you know what to do if there is a flat tire?

- Do you like a sun roof open?

- Do you like to eat in the car?

- Do you like to wear sun glasses in the car?

- Do you like toppings on your ice cream?

- Do you use public bathrooms?

- Did you bring your cell phone and does it have power?

- Do you have a form of identification with you?

- Have you ever been pulled over by a cop?

- Have you ever given money to a stranger on a road trip?

- Have you ever taken a road trip with animals?

- Have you ever went on a vacation alone?

- Have you ever run out of gas?

- If you could move to any place in the world, where would it be?

- If you could travel anywhere in the world, where would you travel?

- If you could travel in any vehicle, which one would it be?

- If you had three things to wish for from a magic genie, what would they be?

- If you have a driver's license, how many times did it take you to pass the test?

- What are you the most afraid of on vacation?

- What do you want to get away from the most when you are on vacation?

- What foods smells bad to you?

- What item do you bring on ever trip with you away from home?

- What makes you sleepy?

- What song would you love to hear on the radio when you're cruising on the highway?

- What travel job would you want the least?

- What will you miss most while you are away from home?

- What is something you always wanted to try?

- What is the best road side attraction that you ever saw?

- What is the farthest distance you ever biked?

- What is the farthest distance you ever walked?

- What is the weirdest thing you needed to buy while on vacation?

- What is your favorite candy?

- What is your favorite color car?

- What is your favorite family vacation?

- What is your favorite food?

- What is your favorite gas station drink or food?

- What is your favorite license plate design?

- What is your favorite restaurant?

- What is your favorite smell?

- What is your favorite song?

- What is your favorite sound that nature makes?

- What is your favorite thing to bring home from a vacation?

- What is your favorite vacation with friends?

- What is your favorite way to relax?

- Where is the farthest place you ever traveled in a car?

- Where is the farthest place you ever went North, South, East and West?

- Where is your favorite place in the world?

- Who is your favorite singer?

- Who taught you how to drive?

- Who will you miss the most while you are away?

- Who if the first person you will contact when you get to your destination?

- Who brought you on your first vacation?

- Who likes to travel the most in your life?

- Would you rather be hot or cold?

- Would you rather drive above, below, or at the speed limited?

- Would you rather drive on a highway or a back road?

- Would you rather go on a train or a boat?

- Would you rather go to the beach or the woods?

TRAVEL BUCKET LIST

1.

2.

3.

4.

5.

6.

7.

8.

9.

10.

NOTES

Made in United States
Troutdale, OR
11/29/2023